Encyclopædia Britannica

Fascinating Facts
Science

PUBLICATIONS INTERNATIONAL, LTD.

Encyclopædia Britannica, Inc.
310 South Michigan Ave.
Chicago, IL 60604

Printed and bound in USA.

8 7 6 5 4 3 2

ISBN: 1-56173-319-9

It's Elemental

Everything in our universe, from people to the air itself, is made up of chemical elements. Mixing the different elements in various ways makes up what we see and feel all around us.

Elements Old and New

Some elements have been known for thousands of years, and they are called by their age-old names. Other elements have only been found recently. Some have been named for famous people— Einsteinium, for example, was named for the great scientist, Albert Einstein. Others were named for places, like Europium, which was discovered in 1901, and Americium, discovered in 1944. Some elements were even named for what they look like. Chlorine, for example, is green in color, and its name comes from the Greek word for "green."

$$E = Mc^2$$

An Element Found Everywhere

Hydrogen is the most abundant element in the universe and the ninth most abundant element (by mass) in the earth's crust and atmosphere. It is present in water, in acids, in all plants and animals, and in most of our food. Hydrogen is invisible and has no taste or smell.

A Very Useful Element

Aluminum is the most common metallic element in the earth's crust. It makes up nearly 8 percent of it. It is used in more ways by people than any other metal. Ground up into a fine powder, it is mixed with oils and used as a paint. When a small amount of aluminum is added to steel, gas holes are eliminated and the material is more solid. It is also used in motion picture film, aluminum foil wrapping, tubes for shaving cream and toothpaste, and other products.

A Noble Gas

Helium was first discovered by the English scientist Joseph Norman Lockyer in 1868 by studying the spectrum of the flame surrounding the sun. It is the second-lightest element and has neither color nor smell. Helium stays in the gaseous state at lower temperatures than any other gas. It only changes into a liquid at –452°F (–268.6°C). Helium is one of the noble, or rare, gases. It is inert, and does not react with other substances. As a result, it is often used to pressurize the very thin walled fuel tanks in spacecraft, which would otherwise collapse under their own weight. Helium is also used to fill lighter-than-air baloons.

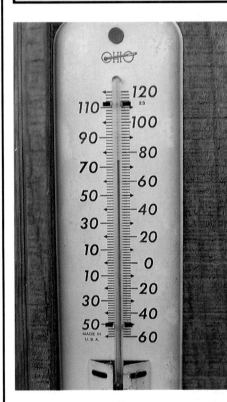

A Liquid Metal ▲

Mercury, otherwise known as quicksilver, is a silvery white metal. It is unusual in that, unlike other metals, it is a liquid at ordinary temperatures. It does not become solid until cooled to its freezing point of –38°F (–39°C). Since mercury expands a good deal when it is heated, it is useful for most thermometers.

Conducting Heat

Most metals are good conductors of heat because the atoms are closely packed in the crystal, and the vibrations involved in the conduction of heat are readily passed on through the structure. If you held an iron rod with one end in a fire, the other end would soon become hot. On the other hand, an iron rod with a wooden handle can be held in the same manner for a long time without getting hot because wood is a poor conductor of electricity.

Working a Metal into Shape ▶

Metals are worked into the shape needed by rolling or hammering them while hot. When the metal has already been rolled into fairly thin sheets (such as for motor vehicle bodies or aluminum saucepans), further heating is unnecessary and shaping is done in a press while cold.

Making a Metal Strong

The strength and hardness of metals can be controlled by alloying and heat treatment. A metal is usually at its softest and weakest when pure and can be strengthened by alloying (mixing) with another metal. For example, pure copper and pure tin are soft and weak, but if the two are melted together they make bronze, a hard, strong alloy.

A Thin Coat of Metal

To prevent rust on steel articles, as well as for improving appearance, thin coatings of metal are made by dipping an object in molten metal. Galvanized steel and fencing wire are coated by being dipped in molten zinc, and "tin cans" are still sometimes made by dipping cans made of very thin steel into molten tin.

At the Heart of the Atom

The nucleus contains most of an atom's mass. It is made up of two kinds of particles called "protons" and "neutrons." Protons have a single positive charge—the kind of charge that marks the positive end of a battery, which is marked with a (+) sign. Neutrons have no electrical charge. Scientists have come to believe that both protons and neutrons are made up of smaller particles called "quarks." Each proton and neutron is made up of three quarks.

Unleashing Nuclear Power

In the 1940s, scientists tried to unleash the energy stored inside the atom. Their plan was simple: If high-speed particles could be shot into the nucleus of an atom, the nucleus would split into two smaller atoms releasing a great amount of energy.

Atomic Energy in Use

There are many uses for the energy that is generated by splitting the atom, or atomic energy. It was used in atomic bombs. It is also used in atomic power plants that produce electricity, for ships and submarines, and even for tiny pacemakers that help people who have heart conditions.

Splitting the Atom

Although it took the work of hundreds of scientists to actually split the atom, the basic idea came from one of the most famous scientists of all time, Albert Einstein. His "Special Theory of Relativity," which he published in 1905, gave him—and others—the idea that energy would be released if atoms were split.

The First Atomic Bomb

When the first atomic bomb was dropped, it sped toward earth just like any other bomb. About 1,850 feet (564 m) off the ground, an explosion was set off inside. Uranium atoms were split, which shot speeding particles of uranium into the mass of uranium inside the bomb, creating a tremendous amount of energy.

Nuclear Devastation

The bomb dropped on the Japanese city of Nagasaki had the force of 21,000 tons of TNT explosive. The blast was so deadly that almost 39,000 people were killed.

The Dangers of Atomic Fallout ▲

An atomic explosion draws dust and dirt into the giant mushroom-shaped cloud that rises over the place where the bomb went off. As this happens, this dirt and dust are covered with radioactive particles, which are carried up into the atmosphere to drift around with the wind. Eventually, they fall back to the earth—far from where the bomb exploded. These deadly radioactive particles are called "fallout."

Modern Nuclear Reactors ▲

In a modern nuclear reactor, uranium is sealed in containers called "rods" that are grouped together. These containers are arranged so that a coolant can flow into the reactor if it gets too hot. Control rods of other materials (such as boron) are used to absorb neutrons and keep the nuclear reaction from turning into an atomic explosion. There is also a thick shield of concrete or steel to contain the radioactivity.

A Nuclear Accident

In 1979, there was an accident at the Three Mile Island nuclear plant near Harrisburg, Pennsylvania. The core of the plant's reactor suffered a partial meltdown—it was partially destroyed by overheating—releasing radioactive gases into the air. The event led to many changes in the way nuclear power plants are run and to more criticism of atomic power.

In 1986, there was an atomic power accident in what was then the Soviet Union, at Chernobyl, near the large city of Kiev. One day in April, there was an explosion inside the nuclear reactor. A huge cloud of radioactive particles escaped from the reactor, which swept westward and northward, covering much of Europe. Only 31 people were killed in the Soviet Union, but 200,000 were taken from their homes for their own safety. Even worse, millions of people and other creatures were exposed to the possibly deadly radiation that made its way as far away as Scandinavia.

The Study of Substances

Chemistry is the study of substances. People study chemistry for two reasons: To discover what the substances on earth are like, and to try to make new substances that can be useful for mankind.

The Branches of Chemistry

Scientists have divided chemistry into several different branches. Organic chemistry studies carbon-containing substances. Physical chemistry studies chemistry that is linked to physics, the science that deals with matter and energy. Analytical chemistry studies what objects are made of. Structural chemistry studies how atoms are arranged in a substance. Biochemistry studies the compounds and chemical reactions found in living organisms.

Chemicals All Around

The chemical industry uses chemicals—and the discoveries of people who study chemistry—to create products for people to use. The chemical industry began in the 1800s when people wanted new, different-colored dyes for their clothes. Scientists experimented until they found new ways to produce colors that could be used safely and efficiently in the clothing industry. Today, the chemical industry is everywhere we look—from our clothing and our food to the furniture in our homes and the cars we drive.

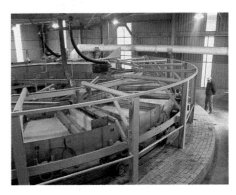

Discovering Gravity

Newton, who is generally considered to be the founder of modern physics, made several very important scientific discoveries. According to a legend that probably is not true, Newton saw an apple drop straight down from a tree branch and decided that the earth attracted the apple. This led him to discover the law of gravity.

All Kinds of Energy

Physics, the oldest of all sciences, is the study of matter and energy. It studies the different states of matter—solid, liquid, gas, and plasma—and their makeup. It also studies light, heat, sound, electricity, and radio waves.

Water changes from liquid to vapor (or gas) when it is heated to boiling in a teapot.

All Living Things

Biology is the study of all living things—from bacteria so small that you cannot see them without a powerful microscope to trees like the giant redwoods of California, which grow up to more than 300 feet (90 m) high.

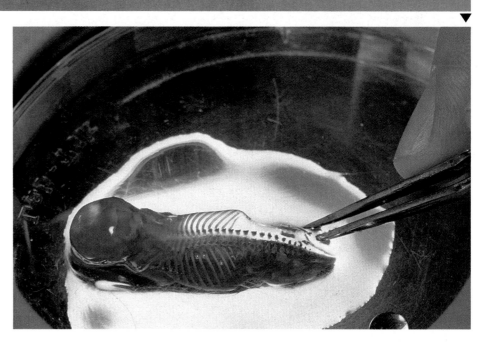

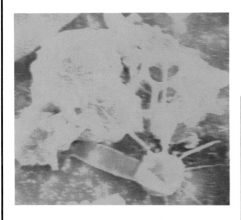

Plants and Animals ▲

Biologists, like all scientists, tend to specialize in one subject or another. Basically, biology is divided into two main branches. Botany is the study of plants, and zoology is the study of animals.

Studying the Stars

Astronomy is the study of the planets and stars. Astronomers not only study what the planets, stars, and galaxies of the universe are like, they also try to answer questions like "How are stars born, and why do they die?" and "How did the universe come about?"

Living by the Stars

Thousands of years ago, people used the stars to figure out the time of year and the time of day in order to know when to plant and harvest their crops. People who could "read" the stars were treated with great respect, often becoming religious and political leaders in the community.

Measuring the Galaxy

An American astronomer named Henrietta Leavitt (1868-1921) was one of the first scientists to think of a way to measure our galaxy. She identified certain stars, called Cepheid variables, which could be used for distance finding. She was able to calculate that Andromeda, another galaxy close to ours, is a little over 2 million light years away.

Babylonian Calendars

As far as we can tell, even cave people studied the stars to learn about weather and seasons. The first serious students of the stars were the ancient Babylonians. They began keeping accurate records of what happened in the sky over 5,000 years ago, and they were able to use their discoveries to create accurate calendars.

A Star Called the Sun

Our sun is exactly the same kind of object as the other stars in the nighttime sky. The only difference between the sun and any of the other stars you see is that it is closer to earth than they are.

Studying Sunspots ▲

Scientists did not get interested in how the sun looked until the first telescopes showed sunspots that could be seen on the surface of the sun from time to time. Galileo, the great scientist of the 1600s, began keeping records of these sunspots in 1610. Scientists have studied them—and the sun—ever since.

Looking at the Sun ▼

The light and energy of the sun come from nuclear reactions deep inside the sun itself. Because huge amounts of heat and light are produced, looking at them can damage your eyes permanently. You should also never look at the sun through a telescope without some kind of protection for your eyes.

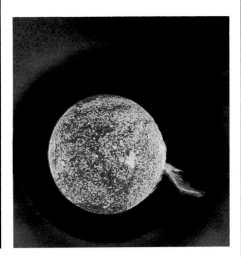

Glowing Arcs of Light ▶

Far to the north—and far to the south—the nighttime sky is sometimes filled with brightly colored lights. These lights flicker across the sky in glowing arcs, in spreading fans of light, or even in bright flashes like giant searchlights. These lights—or *aurora*, as they are called by scientists—are caused by great explosions, or "flares," on the surface of the sun. When a flare takes place, millions of small, electrically charged particles are shot into space. When they reach earth, they bump into the atoms of the air. These tiny collisions produce the light of the aurora.

Catching the Lights

In the northern half of the globe, you can best see the Northern Lights around Hudson Bay in Canada, in northern Scotland, and in Norway and Sweden. The Southern Lights are best seen from Antarctica, which is why few people have ever seen them.

A Very Big Sun

The sun is almost 864,900 miles (1,390,000 km) in diameter, which is around ten times bigger than Jupiter, the biggest planet, and about 109 times bigger than Earth. Even though the volume of the sun is almost 1,300,000 times as great as the volume of the earth, the amount of material inside the sun—its mass, as scientists call it— is only about 333,000 times as great as the earth's. This means that the matter inside the sun is really only $1/4$ as dense as the matter inside the earth.

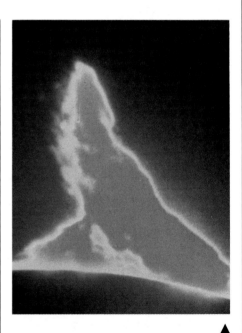

The Sun's Cool Spots

Sunspots are large markings that appear from time to time on the surface of the sun. They look dark to us because they are thousands of degrees cooler than the parts of the sun around them. The sizes and numbers of these spots change over time, but no one knows why this happens. Sunspots seem to reach a peak every 11 years or so; then their number and size decrease for six years before starting to increase again.

That's Very Hot!

The surface of the sun usually runs about 10,800°F (6,000°C). Scientists believe that the center of the sun is a little more than 25,000,000°F (or 14,000,000°C).

Inside the Sun

The sun is a ball of hot gas, with no solid or liquid center at all. It is mostly made up of hydrogen gas, along with helium and small amounts of a few other elements. There are no solids because the sun is so hot that even iron is present as a gas.

The Color of the Sun

Particles in our atmosphere change how the sun looks to us on any given day. It may look white, or yellow, or even red. Scientists have more exact ways to study and label stars and suns. They put stars on a scale that ranges from bluish-white to red. On this scale, our sun is yellow.

A Halo Around the Sun

The corona is the part of the sun's atmosphere that is farthest away from the sun itself. It actually looks like a glowing white halo around the sun. It is made up of electrically charged particles that are only $1/7$ as hot as the center of the sun itself.

Stars of All Sizes

Scientists classify stars by size and density, from giant stars down to tiny neutron stars that are only 12 miles (20 km) in diameter. On this scale, our sun is called a "dwarf."

Our Ever-burning Sun

Scientists believe that the sun has been sending out heat and light for about five billion years. They expect it to go on for another five billion years or so before it finally burns itself up.

◄ Seeing the Moon

The moon has no light of its own; it shines only because it reflects the sun's light. As the moon turns on its axis and travels around the earth, each side of the moon has two weeks of darkness and two weeks of light. When the moon comes between the earth and the sun, the side that is always turned toward the earth is in darkness and is invisible to us. We call this the "new moon."

A Lunar Eclipse ▼

Sometimes the moon is on the opposite side of the earth to the sun. When this occurs, it may move into the earth's shadow, forming a lunar eclipse.

A Solar Eclipse

A solar eclipse occurs when the moon passes between the sun and the earth and blocks out the sun's light.

The Dark Side of the Moon

One of the curiosities about our moon is that one side of it—the side we call the "dark side of the moon"—is always facing away from us, even though it receives more sunlight than the side we face. This is especially strange, since the moon turns around and around in space, just the way the earth does. The moon turns around once in almost exactly the same length of time as it takes for it to move around the earth. As a result, it always shows us the same side.

Craters on the Moon ▲

The moon's craters are giant holes or dents. Some are quite small, but they average about 4,900 feet (1,500 m) across. Most of them were made by meteors striking the moon from space. Others have rings around them, perhaps because they were volcanoes at one time.

Our Spotted Moon ◀

The dark spots on the moon—called *maria* or "seas"—have few craters. Scientists believe that these seas are made of lava from volcanoes. The lava probably filled in the craters in that area and left a dark "stain" on the moon's surface.

A Mistaken Planet

In 1972, scientists announced that there was another planet, called Planet X, beyond Pluto. Within a short time, however, it was clear that no such planet actually existed.

Real Moon Rocks

The "moon rocks" brought back by American astronauts gave scientists a real first-hand look at what the moon was actually made of. They learned that the moon was chemically different than the earth. This discovery convinced scientists that the moon was not a part of the earth that broke away.

Our Sun's Planets

There are nine major planets in our solar system. Each of them moves around our sun in its own orbit. In order of their distance from the sun they are: Mercury, Venus, Earth, Mars, Jupiter, Saturn, Uranus, Neptune, and Pluto.

Fiery Mercury ▲

Because Mercury is so close to the sun, it takes far less time to complete its trip around the sun. As a result, its year is only 88 days—about as long as one of the seasons we have on Earth. Mercury turns very slowly, so that each of its days lasts almost 180 of our Earth days. Mercury's position near the sun also gives it extremely high temperatures. Because Mercury is so small, its gravity is so weak that it cannot even hold the gases of its atmosphere close to the planet.

The Morning Star

Venus's path around the sun is inside Earth's path, so the planet appears to us as a morning or evening star, rising just before or setting just after the sun. In some places, Venus "rises" as much as three hours before dawn and "sets" three hours after sunset. Because it is so bright, people often think of it as a star rather than a planet.

Beautiful to Look At ▲

People of ancient times named Venus after the Roman goddess of love, because they thought the planet looked so beautiful. The surface of the planet is anything but beautiful. In fact, it has one of the most hostile environments in our solar system. Its atmosphere is 96 percent carbon dioxide, and its top layer is made up entirely of dangerous sulfuric acid. Chemical reactions in the atmosphere create lightning and other electrical disturbances all the time. And, the temperature on the surface is around 860°F (560°C)—hotter than most fires.

Our Sister Planet ◄

Mars is so much like Earth that it is often called our "sister planet." It is close to Earth in size and distance from the sun. It also has a temperature closer to ours than other planets. Mars even has an atmosphere of sorts. The Martian day is about the same length as ours, although a year on Mars is almost twice as long as one of Earth's years.

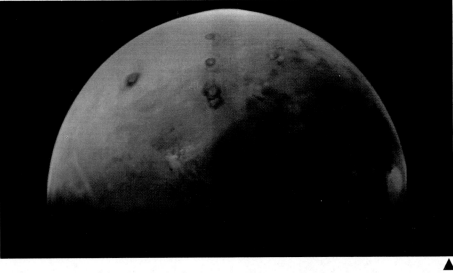

The Red Planet

Mars often appears red in color because of the orange sands that cover its surface. It looks red even to people looking at it without telescopes. This color led people to name the planet after Mars, the Roman god of war who was associated with the red color of blood.

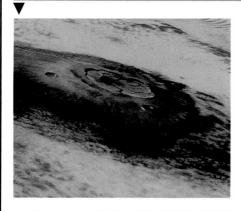

The Last Planet Discovered

Pluto, the ninth planet from the sun, was discovered in 1930 by an American scientist working in Flagstaff, Arizona. As they had done with the discovery of Neptune, scientists used mathematical calculations to predict where it would be.

Moons Big and Small

Saturn has 21 separate moons. They range in size from little moons barely 50 miles (80 km) in diameter up to the largest one, Titan, which is 3,170 miles (5,100 km) in diameter. Titan is so big that it even has its own atmosphere. It would not be nice to breathe this air, since it is made up of nitrogen and the deadly poison, cyanide.

Is There Life on Mars?

In the 1800s, Italian astronomer Giovanni Schiaparelli discovered dark markings on Mars. He called these markings *canali*, which was erroneously translated as "canals" instead of "channels." As a result, people thought that since the planet seemed to have water, it might very well have life of some kind. Later astronomers even thought the bands of color were plants. These observations led people to think that, of all the other places in our solar system, the most likely place for life was Mars.

Jupiter's Unpleasant Climate

Like many other planets, Jupiter has a hostile environment. It is mostly liquid hydrogen, with a solid core deep within the planet. Its huge atmosphere is made of hydrogen with clouds of ammonia. The outer layer of that atmosphere is just about all that we can see of Jupiter from the outside. It also has unpleasant temperatures. The outer atmosphere may be as cold as –202°F (–130°C). Near the planet's center, the temperature probably reaches 45,000°F (25,000°C).

The Rings of Saturn

Saturn, the sixth planet from the sun, has a system of rings around it. Until recently, people thought that Saturn was the only planet with rings. Now, scientists know that both Jupiter and Uranus have rings as well, although they are not as large and spectacular as the rings of Saturn. Saturn has seven flat rings surrounding the planet's middle. They are made up of tiny particles, including both grains of dust and pieces of ice that sometimes are as big as small moons.

Experiments on Mars

On July 20 and September 3, 1976, two American space expeditions landed on Mars. These unmanned space ships, called *Viking Landers,* carried out many experiments on the planet's surface. They found no sign of life on the planet, although some experiments gave signs that there might be micro-organisms of some kind in the planet's soil. These and other space program flights convinced scientists that Mars's famous "canals" were an optical illusion caused by shadows of craters and mountains on the planet's surface.

The Largest Planet

Jupiter is the largest of the planets in our solar system. It was named after Jupiter, the most powerful and greatest of the Roman gods. Jupiter is over 11 times bigger than Earth in diameter and 300 times bigger in mass. In fact, it is bigger than all the other planets put together.

A Man on the Moon

Apollo 11 was the first spacecraft to land humans on the moon. On July 20, 1969, the lunar module Eagle, carrying Neil Armstrong and Edwin Aldrin, landed in the area known as the Sea of Tranquility. Armstrong became the first man to set foot on the moon with the words, "That's one small step for a man, one giant leap for mankind." Together with Aldrin, Armstrong spent about two hours outside the spacecraft, taking photographs, setting up scientific experiments, and collecting rock samples.

Satellite Firsts

The first unmanned satellite was Sputnik 1. It was launched by the Soviet Union on October 4, 1957. It was soon followed by Sputnik 2 in November of 1957. The second satellite carried the dog Laika, which was the first living creature to orbit Earth. The first American satellite, Explorer I, was launched in January 1958.

Spending Time in Space

Skylab was a 99-ton (90-tonne) orbital laboratory, observatory, and workshop. Beginning in May of 1973, three crews of astronauts spent long periods of time in Skylab. The first crew stayed 28 days, the second, 59 days, and the third, 84 days. All the astronauts returned from these long spaceflights fit and well.

Studying the Moon ▲

Five more manned moon landings followed Apollo 11. In all, the Apollo astronauts brought back 848 pounds (385 kg) of lunar soil and rocks and an enormous quantity of information that is still being studied by scientists.

A Very Long Journey

In 1972, the United States launched Pioneer 10 on a 620-million-mile (1-billion-kilometer) voyage to Jupiter. After its encounter with the planet, Pioneer headed out of the Solar System, which it left in June 1983, when it was nearly 3 billion miles (5 billion kilometers) from the sun. Just in case it eventually encounters intelligent beings from other worlds, it carries a plaque showing human beings and their planet Earth.

Another Type of Space Exploration ▲

A new era in space exploration began on April 12, 1981, when the American space shuttle first went into orbit. It was the first reusable spacecraft that was able to fly back from space and land like an aircraft. Mainly used to launch satellites, the shuttle flights also carried specially designed payloads. One was Spacelab, a reusable space laboratory built by the European Space Agency.

Artificial Satellites

There are many different kinds of artificial satellites. *Communications satellites* are used for broadcasting, telephone, and radio. *Weather satellites* are helpful in weather forecasting. *Earth survey satellites* detect mineral deposits, diseased crops, and sources of pollution, and aid in the making of maps. *Military satellites* are used for reconnaissance and intelligence gathering. *Astronomical satellites,* which are observatories in space, orbit above the blanketing layer of the earth's atmosphere.

Revolutionizing Long-distance Travel

HOTOL (Horizontal Take-off and Landing) is intended to be a cross between an airplane and an orbital spacecraft. Its designers hope that it will revolutionize long-distance flights around the world. For example, a journey from London, England, to Sydney, Australia, could take as little as 40 minutes.

When Sparks Fly

If an object is highly charged with electricity, tiny particles of electricity may jump off of it. These electrons, as they are called, actually form a spark. That spark is nothing more than the glowing path made by millions of electrons as they jump through the air.

Letting Electricity Flow

In the world of electricity, a conductor is a medium that electricity flows through quite easily. Water is an excellent conductor of electricity— which is why you are always told not to swim during a thunderstorm. Most metals are also good conductors of electricity.

Flashes of Lightning

Lightning is really nothing more than electricity. Scientists believe that lightning is produced when tiny particles of ice and drops of water inside a cloud are tossed around and knocked against each other by the wind. When they rub against one another, they produce an electrical spark, sending lightning down from the cloud.

Curbing the Flow of Electricity ◄

An insulator is a medium that does not conduct electricity well. Rubber, glass, plastic, and dry air resist the flow of electricity and can be used to insulate objects from electrical flow.

Magnet Mystery

In 1820, Danish scientist Hans Oersted discovered that a magnetic compass needle would swing in a different direction when an electric current was brought near it. This led to the invention of the electromagnet (electrical wire wound around a piece of iron), which can be turned on and off.

A scrap yard crane is an electromagnet that can lift a heavy load.

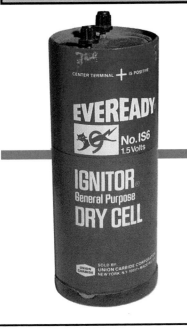

Inside a Battery

Batteries are simple devices. They consist of two or more "cells" (a flashlight battery usually has two to three). The simplest cells are made up of plates of two different kinds of metal, which are kept in salty or acid liquid. When the two plates are connected by a wire, electrical current flows between them.

Letting Electricity Pass

An electrical circuit is a path going from one place to another that allows electricity to pass through it. The "path" is usually made of metal wire, since it conducts electricity very well.

Switching On and Off

An electrical switch is simply a device that interrupts the flow of electricity. It usually does this by creating a gap in the wiring of the circuit. This keeps the electricity from flowing all the way through the circuit until the switch is closed again.

Keeping a Check on Electricity

When electricity is used, there is always the chance that too much electrical power will pass through the wires of the electrical circuit. If this happens, the wires can become too hot and start a fire. To protect against this danger, fuses are placed in the electrical circuit. A *fuse* is nothing more than a short length of a wire that melts very easily. This way, if the wires on the electrical circuit start to get too hot, the metal in the fuse will melt and break the circuit before the main wires get too hot and start a fire. In many homes, fuses have been replaced by circuit breakers—simple switches that automatically turn off when the power passing through a circuit gets too great.

Bringing Electricity to Your Home

Electricity is first made in huge power plants. It flows through a switchgear, which controls its flow and can cut it off if there are any problems along the miles of wires ahead. From here, it goes to a transformer, which increases the pressure so that it can be sent over long distances. High voltage lines then carry the electricity to an area near to where it will be used. The power goes on to a substation, where other transformers reduce the electrical pressure (or "voltage" as it is called), so that it can be safely used. Finally, it is delivered over other wires to your home, business, store, and every other place that uses it.

Back and Forth

Alternating current (AC) flows back and forth in two different directions. The electrical current switches directions so quickly that there is not even the slightest flicker in a light connected to it. Alternating current is used in most of North America because it is easy to send over long distances and because little electricity is wasted as it travels.

Hoover Dam in Colorado produces hydroelectric energy.

Power Plant Particulars ◄

There are two main kinds of power plants. *Thermal plants* use steam turbines to drive generators to make electricity. The steam to drive these turbines comes from burning fuel like oil or coal or even from a nuclear reactor. *Hydroelectric plants* use falling water from a waterfall or dam to drive the turbines. The difficulty with hydroelectric plants is finding a suitable location—they must be built where the water flow is suitable and where they would be close to the towns or factories that need the power.

Measuring Electricity

We measure electric pressure—the amount of electricity flowing through a circuit—in volts. In the United States, most circuits in our homes are set up to run with 110 volts; heavy-duty circuits for washing machines, dryers, and dishwashers are set to have 220 volts. In Great Britain, homes use between 200 and 250 volts.

Generating Electricity

A *generator* is a simple device for making electricity. The very first one was made in 1831 by Michael Faraday, an English scientist. Faraday moved a magnet close to a coil of wire, discovering that this action made electrical current flow through the wire. Ever since, generators, or *dynamos,* as they are sometimes called, have been used to make electricity for everything from homes to ships.

Let It Shine

Light helps us see in two different ways. First, many objects, such as the sun, stars, flames of a fire, and even light bulbs, send out light of their own. More often, we see things because they reflect the light that is shining on them from some other source of light—a lamp, the sun, and so on.

Light's Radiation

Light is actually a kind of radiation. It is different from other radiation in the way that it can be seen by the human eye. Scientists generally identify light as electromagnetic radiation with a wavelength between that of cosmic rays and radio waves.

Partial Light

A translucent object allows only some of the light to pass through. You generally see only shadows or just a general brightness rather than the actual shapes, colors, and surfaces of objects outside.

Absorbing the Light

An opaque substance absorbs or reflects all of the light falling on it. This means that it is impossible to see through an opaque object.

Spectrum Reflections

The color of an object depends on which part of the spectrum it reflects. Most objects reflect some colors and absorb others. Something green looks that color because it reflects most of the light in the green part of the spectrum.

Just Passing Through ▶

An object is transparent when all of the light falling on it is able to pass through it entirely.

Bouncing Off a Surface ◄

Reflection is light bouncing off a surface. The word *reflection* comes from a Latin word that means "bending back." Light that strikes an object bends back in exactly the same way that a wave bounces back from the side of a bathtub or from a rocky cliff.

Changing Directions

In 1621, a Dutch scientist named Willebrord Snell discovered that the direction of light changes when it passes from one transparent substance to another. When light passes from air to glass, it bends or "refracts." It also refracts when it passes from air to water. This happens because the speed of light is different as it goes through each substance. It is fastest going through air.

A Spectrum of Light ▲

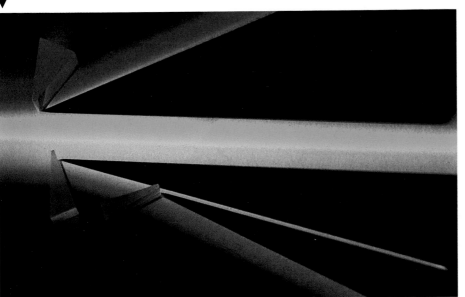

Back in the 1600s, Sir Isaac Newton discovered that white light actually has the whole rainbow of colors in it. That rainbow, which is called the "spectrum," has red, orange, yellow, green, blue, indigo, and violet light in it. When white light (the kind that comes to us from the sun or from a regular light bulb) passes through a prism—a specially shaped piece of glass—it breaks down into these seven colors. A similar phenomenon occurs when light passes through water—which is why you see a rainbow after it rains on a sunny day.

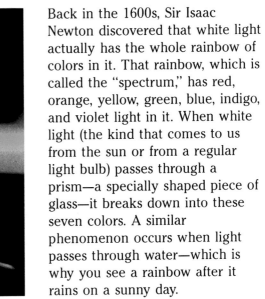

Traveling in Waves ▲

One of the main effects of light is *polarization.* It is best explained by thinking of light as traveling in waves, like ripples, along a rope. If you shake the rope quickly—up and down, side to side, or at an angle—the ripples will travel down the length of the rope. But, if you try to shake a rope that passes between upright sticks, you would only be able to shake it up and down—not side to side. When you coat a piece of glass or plastic with a chemical called herapathite (or a chemical like it), you make the light that passes through the glass or plastic move only in certain directions. This helps make the light less bright, which is why polarized plates are used in making sunglasses and scientific instruments.

Speed of Light

Light travels at a speed of 186,000 miles (300,000 km) per second when it travels in outer space or in an area without air to slow it down. (Light, as you know, travels at different speeds, depending on what it is traveling through. It would be slower through water, glass, or other substances.)

Well-traveled Light ▲

The light that comes to us from the sun (about 93,150,000 miles, or 150,000,000 km, away from us) takes about eight minutes to get here. In a single year, light travels 5,880,870,000,000 miles (9,470,000,000,000 km).

Powerful Lasers ◄

Lasers can send an intense beam over long distances because they are different from regular light in one important way. Ordinary light contains waves vibrating in several different directions. Lasers are *coherent*—all of their waves are vibrating in the same direction at the same time. This makes them powerful and intense—able to do everything from burn their way through metal to "read" the messages coded onto the surface of a CD disc.

To Make a Picture

Photography film is coated with crystals of silver bromide. Energy from light is absorbed by these crystals. As this happens, they are changed so that when the film is developed, the crystals that have been struck by light will react differently from those that have not been struck by light. This accounts for the different colors and shapes that you see in the finished picture.

Traveling by Waves

The term *radiation* comes to us from the Latin word *radius* meaning "beam" or "ray." In science, radiation is the term used for anything that travels by waves—light, heat, X rays, or even cosmic rays.

Very Short Waves

X rays are electromagnetic waves that have wavelengths between $1/10$ of a nanometer and 100 nanometers. (A *nanometer* is 1-billionth of a meter, about 0.000000039 of an inch.)

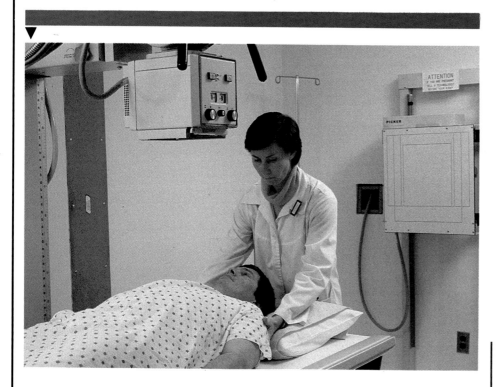

Valuable X Rays

X rays pass through many kinds of materials that reflect light. When an object is exposed to X rays, we can often see right inside. When a broken arm is placed between a source of X rays and a piece of photographic film, the X rays pass right through a person's clothing and skin to show us a picture of a dark shadow that is actually the person's bone. As you probably know, X rays are very valuable in medicine.

Sunlight and Ultraviolet Light

Ultraviolet rays have a longer wavelength, beginning where X rays leave off and extending up to almost 400 nanometers. Sunlight contains ultraviolet rays, which is beneficial to us since these rays help our bodies produce Vitamin D.

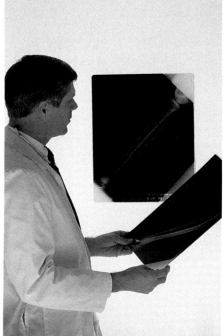

This doctor is studying an X ray to determine the extent of an injury.

From Violet to Red

Radiation Spectrum

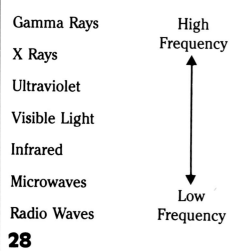

Gamma Rays

X Rays

Ultraviolet

Visible Light

Infrared

Microwaves

Radio Waves

High Frequency

↑

↓

Low Frequency

Visible light is made up of radiation with wavelengths that are a little longer than those of ultraviolet rays. It runs from about 400 nanometers, which is the color violet, up to about 740 nanometers, the color red.

28

Colors of Decreasing Wavelengths

▼

The colors that we see through a spectrum or in a rainbow are simply light waves arranged in order of decreasing wavelength: Red, orange, yellow, green, blue, and violet.

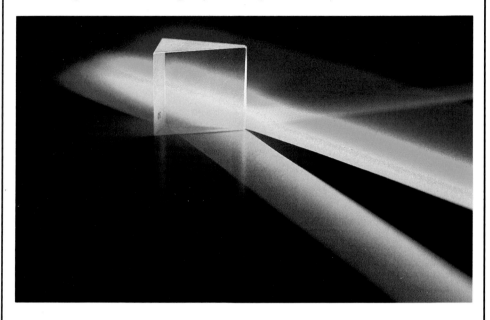

This rainbow in Hawaii is a beautiful sight.

▼

Feeling the Sun's Heat

Infrared rays are longer than those of visible light, running from about 740 nanometers up to 100,000 nanometers. Short infrared waves can travel through mists and clouds that normally stop visible light. Longer infrared waves are felt as heat, which is why the sun's light feels hot to us.

Radar, microwaves, radios, and televisions all use electromagnetic waves to send signals or perform tasks. The waves used in microwave ovens, for example, are about 4.7 inches (12 cm) in length. The ones used for television broadcasting are a little over two yards (two meters) in length. Radio broadcast waves are the longest of all. They are about ⅔ of a mile (1 km) in length.

Radio Waves

When Guglielmo Marconi showed the world his first wireless "radio" in 1896, it made use of electromagnetic waves to send sound from place to place. Marconi's device was simple. It had a coil connected to a battery, which caused high voltage across two metal spheres. Because of the presence of electricity in the spheres, a stream of sparks jumped across the gap between them whenever Marconi tapped an electrical switch. This stream of sparks sent vibrations, or oscillations, up an antenna— and out into the atmosphere.

Beware of Sunburn

Sunburn occurs when too much ultraviolet light comes in contact with the skin. This can lead to more than just redness and discomfort, since scientists now believe that long exposure to ultraviolet light can cause skin cancer.

Dangerous Waves

The beta rays that come from radioactive materials are extremely dangerous. They can cause burning as well as skin cancer. Gamma rays (the shortest waves of all) and X rays can cause even more damage. In small doses, they are often used to kill dangerous cells, like cancer cells, within the body. Long contact with them, however, can kill healthy cells and cause permanent damage to the body.

Radio Wave Discoveries

Radio waves have helped uncover many unusual things. One of these is a *pulsar*, a tiny, heavily condensed neutron star. Another is the remains of *supernovas*, huge explosions in which giant stars blew themselves up. They have also helped scientists discover galaxies almost 500 million light years away. They even helped scientists discover *quasars*, objects that appear something like stars but are much farther away and have vast amounts of energy.

Receiving Radio Waves ▲

Radio waves get weaker and weaker as they cover great distances. A radio or TV program that is being broadcast over a long distance needs to be received and rebroadcast at several stops along the way in order to be received well. Scientists have solved this problem by using communications satellites above the surface of the earth. Signals are sent up to these satellites, which then beam down to exactly where they are to go—without lots of stops, towers, or radio equipment along the way.

Carbon-14 Dating

All living things contain particles of the element carbon in the form of carbon-12. However, there is always a tiny amount of radioactive carbon, called carbon-14, present in all living things. As time goes on, this carbon-14 breaks down. It takes a long time to do this—about 10,000 years or so—but, once a plant or animal dies, carbon-14 breaks down steadily enough for scientists to measure exactly how much of it has disappeared over time. In this way, scientists can figure out how old something is. Carbon-14 dating has helped scientists discover the age of everything from cave paintings to fossils.

Radio Telescopes ▶

Until recently, most astronomers worked with giant optical telescopes. Now, they use radio telescopes to send out radio waves in order to detect radio waves coming to us from the sun, the planets, the stars, or other bodies in space. Since these radio telescopes are more sensitive and more accurate than old-fashioned telescopes—and can identify objects farther away—scientists have found objects in space that they did not know existed.

Reflecting Radio Waves

In 1902, Arthur E. Kennelly and Oliver Heaviside discovered that there was a layer of *ionization* or electrified particles, high above the earth's surface. This layer acts as a mirror to reflect radio waves back to the earth instead of having them go off into space. Because of this layer of ionization, radio waves can be sent from North America to Europe.